PHYSICAL SCIENCE

MICROWORLDS

Unlocking the Secrets of Atoms and Molecules

Anna Claybourne

Rourke
Publishing LLC
Vero Beach, Florida 32964

www.rourkepublishing.com

PHOTO CREDITS: p. 34: The Art Archive/Corbis; p. 27: A. Barrington Brown/Science
Photo Library; p. 37: Jared Cassidy/ istockphoto.com; p. 4: Teyler Derden/istockphoto.com;
p. 24: Kenneth Eward/Biografx/Science Photo Library; p. 40: Chris Fairclough/
CFWImages.com; p. 43: Victor Habbick Visions/Science Photo Library; pp. 10, 26, 35:
istockphoto.com; p. 7: Tony Latham Photography/Getty Images; p. 14: Library of Congress;
p. 29: Steve Lovegrove/ istockphoto.com; p. 9: Carmen Martinez/ istockphoto.com;
p. 15: Prof. Erwin Mueller/Science Photo Library; p. 5: NASA; p. 33: Skip O'Donnell/
istockphoto.com; pp. 21, 31: Ed Parker/EASI-Images/ CFWImages.com; p. 16: David
Philips/istockphoto.com; pp. 6, 18: Photodisc; p. 41: Roger Ressmeyer/Getty Images;
p. 13: Ron Rocz/CFWImages.com; p. 25: Audrey Roordra/istockphoto.com; p. 32: Kim
Sayer/Corbis; p. 38: Paul Vasorhelyi/ istockphoto.com; p. 19: Kirill Zdorov/istockphoto.com.

Cover picture shows an illustration of atoms and molecules [Jose Antonio Nicoli
Andonie/istockphoto.com].

Produced for Rourke Publishing by Discovery Books
Editors: Geoff Barker, Amy Bauman, Rebecca Hunter
Designer: Ian Winton
Cover designer: Keith Williams
Illustrator: Stefan Chabluk
Photo researcher: Rachel Tisdale

Library of Congress Cataloging-in-Publication Data

Claybourne, Anna.
  Microworlds : unlocking the secrets of atoms and molecules / Anna Claybourne.
      p. cm. -- (Let's explore science)
  Includes index.
  ISBN 978-1-60044-606-1
 1. Atoms--Juvenile literature. 2. Molecules--Juvenile literature. 3. Matter--Constitution--
Juvenile literature. 4. Matter--Properties--Juvenile literature. I. Title.
  QC173.16.C53 2008
  539.7--dc22
                              2007020113

Printed in the USA

CONTENTS

chapter one

Introducing Atoms and Molecules

Think about a clear, fresh glass of water. What is the water made of? The answer is **atoms** and **molecules**. A single glass of water contains millions and millions of them. Each one is too small to see by itself.

▶ *You can't see them, but there are many millions of tiny atoms and molecules in this glass of water.*

What Are Atoms and Molecules?

All things are made of these tiny bits, or **particles**. Atoms are like tiny balls. Molecules are groups of atoms joined together. All the stuff around us is made of atoms and molecules. Water, metal, plastic, wood, air, and even living things are all made of atoms and molecules.

▲ *All the stars, moons, and planets in space are made up of atoms and molecules—including our own planet, Earth.*

Matter

Scientists have a name for all this stuff. They call it **matter**. The different kinds of matter are known as **materials**. For example, water, wood, metal, plastic, and stone are all materials.

HOW MANY?

It takes a lot of atoms and molecules to make matter. One cup (8 ounces/240 milliliters) of water contains about 24,000 billion billion (24,000,000,000,000,000,000,000) atoms.

▲*The water in this river can flow and swirl. The metal and concrete bridges are fixed and firm.*

The Way Things Are

Think about that glass of water again. What can you do with water? You can slosh it, stir it, or swirl it around. You can drink it. You can pour it through your fingers.

But you can't do these things with a metal spoon. A metal spoon is hard, and it keeps its shape. Metal and water are both made from atoms and molecules. But they are completely different. How can that be?

Differences

There are many types of atoms. When different atoms join together, they make different types of molecules. Different materials are made up of different atoms and molecules. This makes them behave in different ways.

This book is about what atoms and molecules are and how they make up the amazing, ever-changing world around us.

▲Food is made from atoms and molecules. So are all living things, including humans.

chapter two

All About Atoms

So if everything is made of atoms, what exactly is an atom? What is it like, and what is it made of?

Take a Closer Look

Atoms may be small, but they are made up of parts that are even smaller. At the center is the **nucleus**. The nucleus is made of protons and neutrons.

Atoms also have other parts called **electrons**. The electrons whirl around the nucleus very quickly.

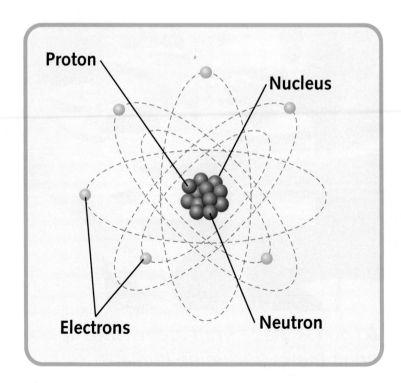

Proton

Nucleus

Electrons

Neutron

▶ *The main parts of an atom.*

Large and Small

There are many different types of atoms. They are all tiny, but some are bigger than others.

For example, a helium atom is a small atom. It has a nucleus made of two protons and two neutrons. It has two electrons zooming around the nucleus. A carbon atom is bigger. It has a nucleus made of six protons and six neutrons. It also has six electrons.

Many atoms are even bigger than this, but they all have the same basic shape and parts.

▶ *Simple diagrams of helium and carbon.*

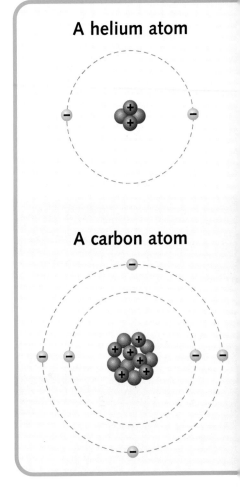

A helium atom

A carbon atom

▼ *Oxygen atoms are another type of atom. They are found in the air we breathe.*

Atomic Numbers

Scientists need to label the different types of atoms, so they know which is which. For this reason, they give atoms numbers.

These are known as atomic numbers. The atomic number depends on how many protons an atom has. For example, oxygen has eight protons. So its atomic number is 8.

▲ *This scientist is looking at a model of a group of different types of atoms.*

Mass Numbers

An atom also has a mass number. This is the number of protons and neutrons added together. An oxygen atom has eight protons and eight neutrons. That makes sixteen. So its mass number is 16.

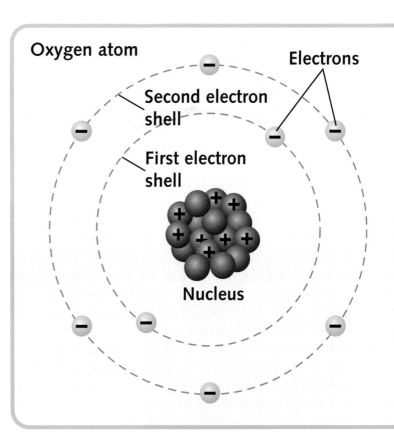

Oxygen atom

Electrons

Second electron shell

First electron shell

Nucleus

►*The first shell holds two electrons. The second shell has space for up to eight electrons. In an oxygen atom, it holds six electrons.*

Electron Shells

The number of electrons in an atom is important, too. The electrons move around in different layers, called electron shells.

The first shell is closest to the nucleus. It holds up to two electrons. The second shell can hold up to eight electrons. There can be more shells, too. An atom has as many shells as it needs to hold all its electrons.

How Small Are Atoms?

It's hard to imagine how small atoms are. One single atom is about one 250-millionth of an inch (0.000000004 inches). That's the same as one ten-millionth of a millimeter across (0.0000001 mm).

Counting Atoms

You could fit more than twenty million atoms into one period on this page. The page itself is about a million atoms thick. If you lined up atoms in a row, you would need fifty million of them to make a line as long as your little fingernail.

EMPTY SPACE

Most of the matter in an atom is in its nucleus. The nucleus takes up a tiny part of the atom. The rest is the space around the nucleus, where the electrons whirl. So an atom is mostly empty space. That means that all the things around us— and our own bodies—are also mostly empty space!

Electron cloud, where electrons are zooming around very quickly.

Nucleus

▲*Gold leaf is one of the thinnest materials you can find. It's about 300 atoms thick. Here it covers the domed roofs of these beautiful towers in Moscow, Russia.*

The Story of Atoms

Atoms are far too tiny for us to see with just our eyes.
So how do we know they are there?

Ancient Greek scientists wondered what things were made of.
Some said everything was made of water or air. But one
scientist, Democritus, said that everything was made of tiny
particles. The particles did not change, and they could not be
broken. He named these particles atoms. The word atom is
Greek for "thing that cannot be split in two."

John Dalton

The scientist John Dalton lived from 1766 to 1844. He found
out much more about atoms. He thought that different
materials must be made up of different types of atoms.
Different atoms must have different numbers of parts. Dalton
is often called "the
father of chemistry."
Chemistry is the study
of what materials are
made of and how they
react to each other.

◀*A portrait of
John Dalton.*

Under the Microscope

Today, we have very strong microscopes. With them, we can actually see atoms. What we can see proves that Democritus and Dalton were right.

►The tiny dots in this picture show where iridium atoms are, or have just been. They are seen under a special microscope.

chapter three

Amazing Elements

An **element** is a material that contains just one type of atom. There are about one hundred different types of atoms altogether. So there are about one hundred elements.

Think of an Element

Lots of materials that you know are elements. For example, silver is an element. It is made of silver atoms. We use silver to make jewelry, silverware, and other things.

▶*A pair of silver rings.*

A silver atom

▶ *A silver atom has forty-seven protons, sixty-one neutrons, and forty-seven electrons.*

Look at the list of elements. How many have you heard of?

The Elements

This list shows ninety-two elements that are found naturally on Earth.

Elements on Earth

Actinium	Fluorine	Neodymium	Selenium
Aluminum	Francium	Neon	Silicon
Antimony	Gadolinium	Nickel	Silver
Argon	Gallium	Niobium	Sodium
Arsenic	Germanium	Nitrogen	Strontium
Astatine	Gold	Osmium	Sulfur
Barium	Hafnium	Oxygen	Tantalum
Beryllium	Helium	Palladium	Technetium
Bismuth	Holmium	Phosphorus	Tellurium
Boron	Hydrogen	Platinum	Terbium
Bromine	Indium	Polonium	Thallium
Cadmium	Iodine	Potassium	Thorium
Cesium	Iridium	Praseodymium	Thulium
Calcium	Iron	Promethium	Tin
Carbon	Krypton	Protactinium	Titanium
Cerium	Lanthanum	Radium	Tungsten
Chlorine	Lead	Radon	Uranium
Chromium	Lithium	Rhenium	Vanadium
Cobalt	Lutetium	Rhodium	Xenon
Copper	Magnesium	Rubidium	Ytterbium
Dysprosium	Manganese	Ruthenium	Yttrium
Erbium	Mercury	Samarium	Zinc
Europium	Molybdenum	Scandium	Zirconium

Important Elements

Elements play a big part in our everyday lives. The gas oxygen is an element, made of oxygen atoms. It is found in the air. Animals must breathe in oxygen to stay alive. Carbon is another important element. It is found in the bodies of living things.

▲*Even fish breathe oxygen. They take it from the water using their gills.*

Some elements are rare. This means they are hard to find. Because of this, they cost a lot of money. They include gold and platinum. Gold was once used to make coins.

►*A computer has a chip like this in it, to make it work. The chip is made of silicon. Silicon is an element.*

Code Names

Scientists give each element its own code name. The code name acts as a symbol for that type of atom. It is made of one, two, or three letters. This makes it quicker and easier to write elements down.

Here are some of the codes:
Oxygen—O
Carbon—C
Silicon—Si
Silver—Ag
Gold—Au

ELEMENT NAMES

Elements get their names in many ways. Helium is found in the Sun. Its name comes from *helios*, the Greek word for "sun."

Gold is a yellow metal. Its name comes from an old word, *gelwa*. This means "yellow."

Xenon is an unusual element. Its name comes from a Greek word, *xenos*, meaning "strange."

Showing Molecules

Like atoms, most molecules are much too small for us to see on their own. But we can draw diagrams and make models of them. This helps us to understand how the atoms are arranged and joined together.

Pictures of Molecules

On a flat page or computer screen, molecules are shown as diagrams. Sometimes, the diagrams show atoms joined together. They look like balls stuck to one other.

▶ *This diagram shows atoms as balls. This is a water molecule.*

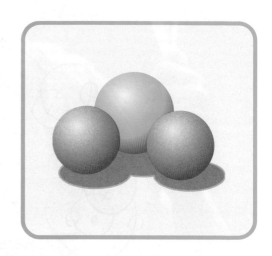

Other diagrams show the atoms as balls joined together with sticks.

3-D Models

Scientists can also build model molecules. Then they use real-life balls and sticks. The balls stand for atoms. The sticks fix them together to make molecules.

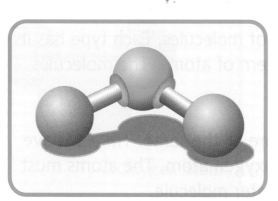

◀ *This is a ball-and-stick diagram of a water molecule (H_2O).*

MOLECULES IN CODE

As you know, each atom has its own code name. For example, the code name for oxygen is O.

Scientists can also use code names, or formulas, to name whole molecules. For example, water is made of two hydrogen atoms and one oxygen atom. The **chemical formula** for this molecule looks like this:

H stands for "hydrogen."

The O stands for "oxygen." It has no number after it. That means there is only one oxygen atom.

The 2 after the H shows that there are two hydrogen atoms.

Millions of Molecules

As you know, there are about one hundred types of atoms. This number has changed as scientists have discovered new elements.

The elements can be arranged in all kinds of patterns. Each different pattern makes a different molecule. In fact, there are millions of types of molecules.

Mini Molecules

We have read that molecules can be different sizes. Some molecules are small. A water molecule (H_2O) has just three atoms. An oxygen molecule (O_2) has just two.

Mega Molecules

Other molecules are much bigger. They can have dozens or hundreds of atoms. For example, carbon atoms can form big molecules. These molecules are called buckyballs. Each buckyball contains sixty carbon atoms. They are joined together in a sphere. It looks like a ball.

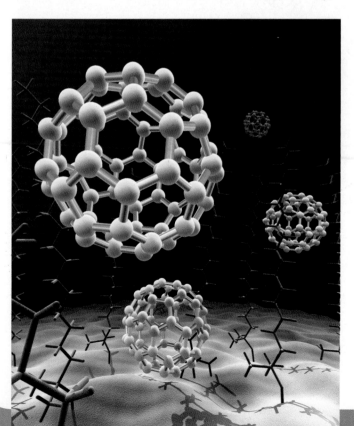

◀ *A "buckyball" carbon molecule.*

▲ *Plastics, such as those used to make waterproof coats and boots, contain polymer molecules.*

Chain Molecules

Some molecules are like chains. More and more atoms can be added. They make a pattern that repeats over and over. These "chain" molecules are called **polymers**. Plastics are made of polymer molecules.

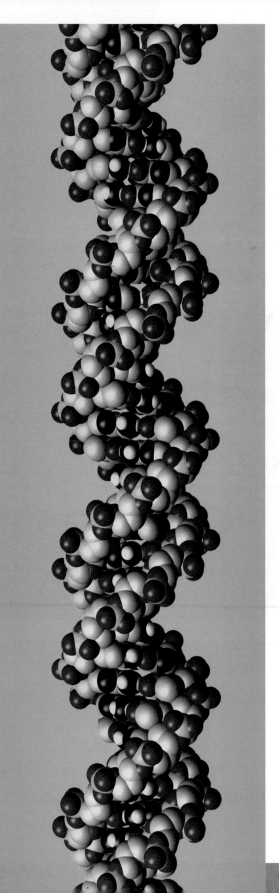

Amazing Molecules

Molecules are in everything. They are all around us, all the time. Most molecules simply make up materials, but some have amazingly useful jobs.

DNA

DNA is short for "deoxyribonucleic acid." This is a very important molecule. It is found inside living things. It is a chain molecule, or polymer. The atoms are arranged in patterns along the DNA chain. These patterns of atoms act as instructions for living things. They tell them how to live and grow.

◀ *A diagram of part of a DNA molecule chain.*

Medical Molecules

Many medicines work because of the shape of their molecules. For example, aspirin is a **painkiller**. Aspirin molecules can lock onto a body **chemical** that makes pain signals. They can lock together because their shapes fit together. This blocks the signals, and the pain stops.

WATSON AND CRICK

In 1953, scientists James Watson and Francis Crick made a great discovery. They figured out the shape of DNA. They used balls and sticks to build a model of the DNA molecule.

Carbon Tubes

Besides buckyballs, carbon atoms can form carbon nanotubes. These molecules are shaped like long tubes. They are light, flexible, and amazingly strong. They are up to one hundred times stronger then steel.

chapter five

Bonding and Reacting

Atoms join together to make molecules. This joining is known as **bonding**. But how do atoms bond together? And why?

Counting Electrons

An atom has electrons zooming around inside of it. The electrons are found in layers, or shells (see page 11).

Atoms like to have a full number of electrons in their outer shell. For example, an oxygen atom has six electrons in its outer shell, but that shell can hold eight. So the oxygen atom will try to find two more electrons to fill the shell.

▶ *Oxygen atom.*

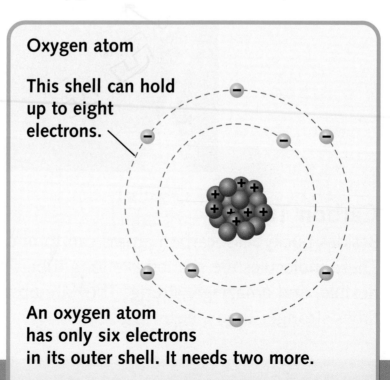

Oxygen atom

This shell can hold up to eight electrons.

An oxygen atom has only six electrons in its outer shell. It needs two more.

Some atoms already have a full outer shell. They are said to be **stable**. They do not need to join with other atoms. Gold is an example. It hardly ever forms molecules. Instead, gold atoms often stay by themselves.

►*Gold is found as pure gold nuggets in the ground. This is because gold is stable. It does not join with other atoms to make new substances.*

Getting Together

Sometimes, atoms bond so that they can share electrons. Then, as long as they stick together, they get the electrons they need. This is called covalent bonding.

Another type of bonding is ionic bonding. This happens when one atom gives electrons to another atom.

Covalent Bonding

In covalent bonding, atoms join to share their electrons. Water molecules are made this way. Here's what happens.

An oxygen atom needs two extra electrons to fill its outer shell. A hydrogen atom needs one extra electron to fill its outer shell.

So an oxygen atom joins with two hydrogen atoms. This gives the oxygen the extra electrons it needs. And, the hydrogen atoms get what they need, too. They share the oxygen's electrons to get one extra electron each.

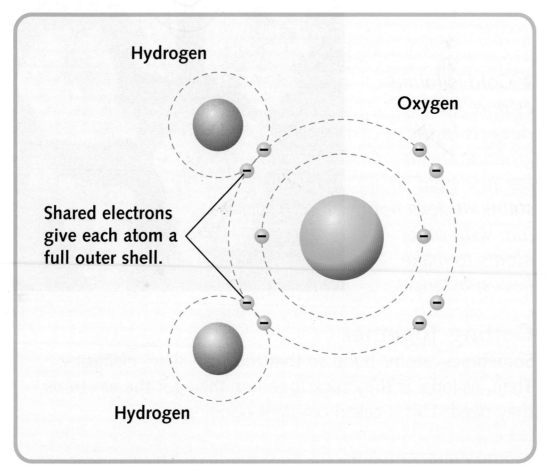

Hydrogen

Oxygen

Shared electrons give each atom a full outer shell.

Hydrogen

▲ *Water molecule.*

▲ *Salt (sodium chloride), which we use on our food, is a common substance found in seawater.*

Ionic Bonding

In ionic bonding, one atom gives electrons to another atom that needs them.

Salt (sodium chloride) molecules are made this way. A sodium atom has a spare electron. A chlorine atom needs one. In salt, the sodium atoms give their electrons to the chlorine atoms.

This changes the atoms. It makes them pull toward each other. They stick together like magnets, making a molecule.

▲ *The dome of the London Planetarium is made of copper. Copper reacts with oxygen in the air to make a molecule called copper oxide. It gives the copper a bright green coating.*

Chemical Reactions

Atoms and molecules aren't locked into the same patterns forever. They can move around, change places, and make new molecules. When this happens, it is called a **chemical reaction**.

The word *chemical* means "a substance made of atoms or molecules." Chemicals often react when put together. For example, if you put sodium and chlorine together, they react. They make sodium chloride molecules.

ALWAYS REACTING

Some atoms are very unstable. They are said to be **reactive**. They react easily and quickly, so they are usually found as part of molecules. Sodium and fluorine are very reactive. If you put fluorine in water, for example, it explodes.

Reactions Everywhere

Chemical reactions take place around us all the time. They happen inside our bodies when we digest food. They happen in cooking when we mix ingredients. A chemical reaction happens when things burn.

When iron meets air and water it causes a chemical reaction. The atoms make a new molecule, iron oxide. We call it rust.

▲ *The ingredients you put into a cake react together when they are mixed and cooked.*

chapter six

Matter and Materials

Matter is all the stuff around us that is made from atoms and molecules. There are millions and millions of different types of matter. They are known as materials.

Using Materials

Since humans first existed, we have been using materials to make our lives easier. The earliest people made tools and machines from stone. This was the Stone Age. After that came the Bronze Age and the Iron Age, when humans learned to use metals. More recently, we have learned to make new materials, such as plastics.

▶These axe heads and arrowheads were carved about 9,000 years ago, during the Stone Age.

▲*Modern materials such as plastics and carbon fiber are used to make sports gear, like this snowboard and helmet.*

Material Words

Several words are used to describe matter and materials. This is what they mean:

Matter: The stuff from which everything is made.

Material: Any type of matter.

Element: A material that is the same throughout, such as gold or silver.

Compound: A substance made of molecules, each of which is made up of two or more different types of atoms. Salt (sodium chloride) is a compound.

Mixture: A material made of different substances mixed together. Air is a mixture of oxygen, nitrogen, and other gases.

Properties of Materials

Different materials have different features and ways of behaving. These are called **properties**. For example, steel is hard. Wool is soft.

Other properties include how strong, stretchy, or flexible (bendy) a material is. What color is it? Is it see-through? Does it float? Does it burn easily? Does it feel warm or cold to touch? Does it **conduct** (carry) **electricity**?

The Right Material

Properties decide how a material is used. For example, a screwdriver has to be strong and hard, so it has a steel tip. But its handle must be easy to grip. So it is made of plastic, wood, or rubber. Concrete is heavy and strong. It works well for building houses but would be useless for making pants.

Can you think of other things that work better when they are made of particular materials? Which materials could you make a good coffee cup out of? Which materials would not make a good cup—and why? Here's a list of materials to consider: wood, cork, cotton fabric, chocolate, china, steel, plastic, sponge, stone.

SOLIDS, LIQUIDS, AND GASES

Many materials can be a **solid**, a **liquid**, or a **gas**, depending on the temperature. For example, water is often a liquid. But below 32°F (0°C), it freezes solid. It becomes ice. Above 212°F (100°C), water boils. It becomes an invisible gas. Solid, liquid, and gas are called the three **states of matter**.

▲ Swimming goggles are made of materials that help them to do their job. The clear plastic lenses let you see through them. The flexible rubber edges and strap hug your head closely.

Inventing Materials

Scientists can now make materials that never existed before. The first plastics, made from plants or oil, were invented in the 1800s. More recent inventions include Teflon nonstick coating for pans, and stretchy fabrics such as Lycra. Kevlar is a super-strong material. It is used to make bulletproof vests and space gear.

▶ *A bulletproof vest made using Kevlar can stop bullets in the space of just two inches.*

ATOM POWER

If an atom is split open, it releases energy. This is called **nuclear fission**. Nuclear power comes from nuclear fission. Unfortunately, this invention has brought problems. It creates dangerous waste. It can also be used to make very powerful nuclear weapons.

▶ In nuclear fission, an atom is broken apart. It releases energy and particles. Some of the particles then split open other atoms.

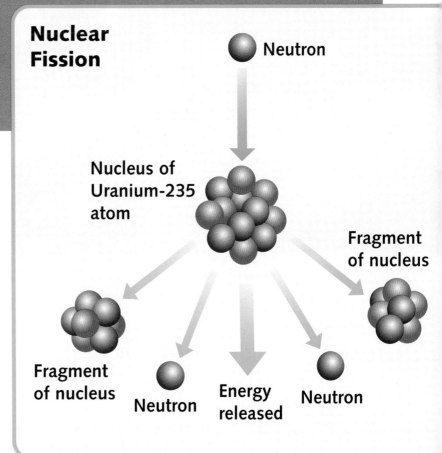

Nuclear Fission

Neutron

Nucleus of Uranium-235 atom

Fragment of nucleus

Fragment of nucleus

Neutron

Energy released

Neutron

Materials For Energy

We use materials to make things. We also turn them into useful **energy**. For example, we burn wood to make heat. Fuel made from oil powers cars and planes. Power stations burn coal, oil, or gas to produce electricity.

▲ *We mine many materials from the ground. Here, a conveyor belt takes a special clay called bauxite from a mine in Australia to a nearby smelter. Aluminum is removed from the heated clay.*

Using Up Materials

We get materials such as rock, oil, wood, metal, and precious stones from nature. But Earth does not have an endless supply of these materials. Some of them are being used up.

Collecting materials can damage the planet, too. For example, we dig under the seabed for oil. This breaks up the seabed, and can kill sea creatures. Chopping down trees for wood destroys forest habitats where animals live.

Making Our Own

Many molecules can be synthesized. This means scientists can make them in the lab. For example, aspirin (see page 26) was first discovered in tree bark, but we do not get it from trees anymore. Most aspirin is synthesized instead.

ATOM SCIENCE

Chemists and physicists are scientists who study matter. They try to find out how atoms and molecules work, how they bond, and how they behave. This helps scientists invent and produce materials. It also helps us understand the universe and where matter came from.

▲ A scientist prepares jars of different chemicals for an experiment.

chapter seven

Into the Future

The science of matter is more important then ever. New materials will help scientists create amazing new technology. We may also discover much more about how matter works.

FUTURE FUSION

Nuclear fusion is a way of joining atoms together to release energy. It is safer than nuclear fission (see page 39). It powers the Sun, making it give off heat and light. Scientists are trying to find a way to make nuclear fusion work on Earth. We could get energy from it.

Nuclear Fusion

Heavy hydrogen (Deuterium nucleus)

Heavy hydrogen (Tritium nucleus)

Neutron

Hydrogen nuclei fuse

Helium nucleus formed

Energy released

Neutron expelled

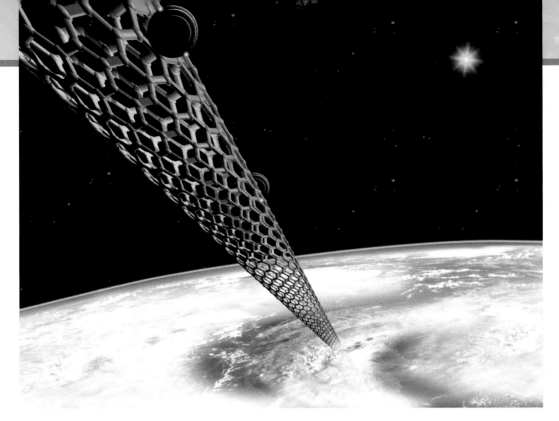

▲ *The space elevator could look like this.*

Carbon Leads the Way

Carbon buckyballs and nanotubes (see page 27) can be used in **nanotechnology**—building tiny machines. These machines could be used to do repairs inside the body or clean up pollution.

Another idea being planned is a space elevator. It would link Earth's surface to a satellite in orbit. Astronauts and supplies could travel up it to space. For a long time, this idea was thought impossible. But carbon nanotubes are so strong and light, they could be used to build it.

Mysteries of Matter

Scientists still do not really know what matter actually is. We know about atoms, and the parts they are made of. But what are they made of? Scientists are working hard to solve these puzzles. When they do, we might find new ways to turn matter into energy. Maybe we will be even able to escape **gravity**.

Glossary

atoms (AT uhms) — tiny particles that make up materials

bonding (BON ding) — when atoms join together to make a molecule

chemical (KEM uh kuhl) — a substance made up of atoms or molecules

chemical formula (KEM uh kuhl FOR myuh luh) — a code used to stand for an atom or molecule

chemical reaction (KEM uh kuhl ree AK shuhn) — when atoms move around and rearrange themselves to make new molecules

compound (KOM pound) — a substance made of molecules made up of two or more different types of atoms

conduct (kuhn DUHKT) — to allow electricity to flow through

DNA (short for deoxyribonucleic acid) (dee en AY) — a molecule found in living things. It stores instructions that tell living things how to live and grow.

electricity (i lek TRISS uh tee) — a form of energy that can flow along wires

electron (i LEK tron) — a tiny particle that flies around the nucleus in an atom

element (EL uh muhnt) — a substance made up of just one type of atom

energy (EN ur jee) — the ability to do work

gas (gass) — a state of matter in which molecules are widely spread out and a substance has no fixed shape

gravity (GRAV uh tee) — the force that causes matter to pull toward other matter

liquid (LIK wid) — a state of matter in which molecules are loosely attached, and substances can flow or be poured

material (muh TIHR ee uhl) — any type of matter

matter (MAT ur) — the stuff that things are made of. Matter is made up of atoms and molecules.

mixture (MIKS chur) — a material made of different substances mixed together

molecule (MOL uh kyool) — a group of atoms joined together

nanotechnology (nan oh tek NOL uh jee) — an area of technology involving making very small objects and machines

nuclear fission (NOO klee ur FISH uhn) — splitting an atom apart to release energy

nuclear fusion (NOO klee ur FYOO zhuhn) — joining atoms together to release energy

nucleus (NOO klee uhss) — the center of an atom, containing protons and neutrons

painkiller (PAYN kil ur) — a medicine that numbs pain, such as aspirin

particle (PAR tuh kuhl) — a tiny bit or part

polymer (POL uh mur) — a type of molecule shaped like a chain made up of repeated sections. A polymer can grow longer and longer as more atoms are added to it.

properties (PROP ur tees) — the qualities or features of matter, such as strength or hardness

reactive (ree AK tiv) — a reactive atom is one that reacts easily with other atoms or substances

solid (SOL id) — a state of matter in which molecules are firmly held together, giving substances and objects a fixed shape

stable (STAY buhl) — a stable atom is one that does not react easily with other atoms or substances

states of matter (states ov MAT ur) — the three main forms in which matter can exist: solid, liquid, and gas

Further Information

Books

Atoms and Molecules. Louise and Richard Spilsbury. Heinemann, 2007.

Looking at Atoms and Molecules. Library of Physical Science (series). Suzanne Slade. Rosen Publishing Group's PowerKids Press, 2007.

Touch It!: Materials, Matter and You. Primary Physical Science (series). Adrienne Mason. Kids Can Press, 2005.

What Are Atoms? Lisa Trumbauer. Children's Press, 2005.

Websites to visit

www.miamisci.org/af/sln/phantom/papercutting.html
The Atoms Family.
This site has papercutting activity to show how small an atom is.

www.bbc.co.uk/schools/ks2bitesize/science/materials.shtml
BBC schools.
This website explores the different properties of materials. It contains interactive activities.

www.nyscience.org/marvelousmolecules/marveloussub.html
New York Hall of Science.
This site shows you lots of marvelous molecules.

www.abpischools.org.uk/resources/solids-liquids-gases/index.asp
Solids, Liquids, and Gases.
Animations show why different materials have different properties.

www.strangematterexhibit.com/
Strange Matter.
Discover the secrets of everyday stuff. This site has plenty of fun activities to try.

Index